How to Create a Secret Society:
A Handbook for Enriching Your College School Experience with Mystery and Fraternity

Produced Martell Books
Edited by Carey Martell

How to Create a Collegiate Secret Society
First Edition Printing, November 8th, 2023
Copyright 2023 Carey R. Martell
    All rights reserved.

ISBN-13: 9798867011512

Published by Martell Books (http://martellbooks.com/)

Table of Contents

How to Create a Secret Society

Prelude: The Allure of Secrecy

The allure of secrecy is a deeply rooted aspect of human psychology and social behavior. Throughout history, secret societies have captured the public imagination, tantalizing with the promise of hidden knowledge, exclusive camaraderie, and sometimes, the power to shape events from behind the scenes. The fascination with what is concealed from the general eye speaks to our inherent desire for a space where we can explore ideas, relationships, and activities unfettered by the broader societal norms.

Why does secrecy allure? At its core, secrecy implies a boundary between those who know and those who do not—those within the circle of trust and those outside it. This demarcation creates a sense of exclusivity, belonging, and identity among its members. It offers an escape from the mundane, a break from the transparency and predictability of everyday life, and a plunge into the mysterious and the esoteric.

In the realm of secret societies, particularly in academic settings such as a college campus, this allure is often magnified by the age-old traditions of academia itself—a world where robes, rites, and rigorous scholarship blend into a fertile ground for clandestine organizations. From the Ivy League's Skull and Bones to the fictional societies in works like Donna Tartt's "The Secret History," the concept of a hidden collective operating on the fringes of collegiate life has a strong pull. It suggests a narrative where the ordinary student can be initiated into a world of ancient lore, sophisticated rituals, and bonds of friendship that promise to last a lifetime.

The appeal of secrecy also lies in its capacity to foster a deep sense of connection among members. Within the confidential confines of a secret society, individuals can share their true selves, away from the watchful eyes of society. The trust required to maintain secrecy becomes a foundation upon which solid relationships are built. Such intimacy is rare in the open, where one's words and actions are often subject to the court of public opinion.

Moreover, secrecy begets curiosity and inquisitiveness. The less we know, the more we want to know. This holds true for both members and non-members of secret societies. For the initiate, each revealed secret peels back a layer of the larger mystery, driving deeper commitment to the group's cause and ethos. For the outsider, the mystery surrounding these societies can lead to a mix of reverence, suspicion, and sometimes, the desire to unmask.

In a college environment, the yearning for a secret society's shrouded experiences might also be linked to the developmental stage of its potential members. College students stand on the threshold of adulthood, seeking to define their identities and their paths in life. A secret society can provide a playground for this exploration—a place where the intensity of youthful idealism can be channeled into creative, intellectual, and social endeavors shielded from external judgment.

However, the allure of secrecy is not without its pitfalls. There exists a fine line between the innocent preservation of privacy and the potential for exclusionary behavior and un-ethical conduct. The power that comes with secrecy can be intoxicating, and without checks and balances, it can lead to abuses. The challenge for any secret society, especially those within the crucible of academia, is to balance the se-ductive pull of the hidden with the ethical imperative to do no harm.

In embracing secrecy, these societies also take on a responsibility. It becomes crucial to ensure that the secret space they create is not just a self-serving enclave but a force for positive influence and mutual support. The tradi-tions and rituals that these societies embrace must, therefore, serve not only to strengthen the bonds among members but also to uphold the values and principles that brought them together.

In conclusion, the allure of secrecy in the formation of secret societies is multifaceted. It satisfies the human cravings for intimacy, the excitement of the unknown, the prestige of exclusivity, and the joy of shared experiences. As long as humanity is drawn to the unexplained and the hid-den, secret societies will continue to form, offering their members a refuge from the world's glare. However, the true art lies in managing the secrets so that they serve a greater good, ensuring that what is whispered in the shadows can withstand the scrutiny of the light.

Historical Overview of Secret Societies

Throughout history, secret societies have captivated the human imagination. From the mystery-shrouded gatherings in ancient civilizations to the clandestine clubs of the modern era, these organizations have played influential roles in the social, political, and cultural narratives of societies worldwide. This chapter delves into the rich tapestry of secret societies, tracing their origins, evolution, and the enduring legacy they have left on the fabric of history.

Beginnings in Antiquity

The roots of secret societies stretch back to antiquity, where mystery cults and brotherhoods were established as a means of preserving sacred knowledge, conducting rites, and fostering bonds beyond the reach of the public eye.
Examples include;

- Eleusinian Mysteries (c. 1600 BCE–392 CE): These were initiatory rituals held annually in honor of the Greek goddesses Demeter and Persephone. They are one of the earliest examples of a secret society, where initiates were bound by a vow of secrecy regarding the esoteric knowledge imparted during the ceremonies.

- Pythagorean Brotherhood (c. 6th century BCE): Founded by the philosopher Pythagoras, this society combined mathematical rigor with mystical teachings. The Pythagoreans were known for their communal lifestyle, secretive practices, and significant contributions to mathematics, music, and philosophy.

Medieval Enigmas

In the Middle Ages, secret societies often emerged within the crevices of religious and political power structures, sometimes as guardians of knowledge during times of persecution, or as groups seeking esoteric wisdom.

- Knights Templar (c. 1119–1312): As a Christian military order, the Templars amassed power and wealth which eventually led to their dissolution and the mythos surrounding their secret knowledge and alleged activities.
- The Assassins (c. 1090–1275): Also known as the Nizari Ismailis, they were a group that practiced political murder and operated covertly. Their shrouded practices contributed significantly to the legend and lore surrounding their name.

The Enlightenment and the Birth of Modern Secret Societies

The Age of Enlightenment gave rise to societies that fostered intellectual exchange and operated under veils of secrecy to protect their members from political and religious persecution.

- Freemasons (c. late 16th–early 17th century): With roots in the stonemason guilds, Freemasonry evolved into a fraternal organization with elaborate rituals. Its members, including numerous influential figures, played key roles in social and political revolutions.
- Rosicrucians (c. early 17th century): Purportedly founded by Christian Rosenkreuz, this society combined elements of mysticism, alchemy, and spiritualism. Although its actual existence is debated, its impact on occult traditions and literature is undeniable.

The Age of Revolution

During the turbulent times of political upheaval, secret societies often became hotbeds for revolutionary thought and action.

- Illuminati (c. 1776–1785): Officially named the Bavarian Illuminati, they sought to promote Enlightenment ideals and oppose religious influence and superstition. Despite their brief existence, their legacy continues to fuel conspiracy theories.

- Carbonari (c. early 19th century): Active in Italy, this secret society was instrumental in orchestrating uprisings aimed at ending foreign rule and establishing constitutional governance.

The 19th and 20th Centuries:
Global Expansion and Diversification

The Industrial Revolution and subsequent global changes saw the proliferation of secret societies across the world, with varied objectives and influences.

- Skull and Bones (c. 1832–Present): Founded at Yale University, this society is known for its powerful alumni. Its secretive nature has led to much public curiosity and speculation about its influence.
- Thule Society (c. 1918–1925): A German occultist group that had a significant, albeit indirect, impact on the rise of Nazi ideology.
- Secret Societies in the Contemporary World
- Today, the influence of secret societies is often discussed in the context of their historical impact and the extent of their power in contemporary politics, finance, and culture.
- Bohemian Club (c. 1872–Present): An exclusive club that hosts an annual gathering at the Bohemian

Grove, attended by some of the world's most power-ful individuals.

- Bilderberg Meeting (c. 1954–Present): An annual private conference of influential figures from North America and Europe, it has become fodder for theo-rists who speculate on the behind-the-scenes orches-tration of global events.

Cultural Representation and Legacy

Secret societies have not only influenced history directly but have also been a staple of cultural expression, inspiring countless works of fiction, film, and conspiracy theories. They continue to fascinate due to their blend of secrecy, power, and the human quest for knowledge and belonging. Literature and Film: Works like Umberto Eco's "Foucault's Pendulum" and movies such as "National Treasure" draw heavily on the mythos surrounding secret societies, blending fact with fiction to create compelling narratives.

Conclusion

Secret societies offer a unique window into the psychologi-cal, sociological, and historical aspects of humanity. Their hidden nature challenges us to consider the unseen forces that shape our world, the allure of the forbidden, and the power of the collective working in the shadows. As long as there is knowledge to be safeguarded, power to be exercised, and the allure of the unknown, secret societies will likely continue to exist, evolve, and intrigue.

The tapestry of history is richer for the presence of secret societies, and the threads they add are as complex as they are compelling. Whether viewed as guardians of ancient wisdom, catalysts for change, or mere gatherings of the like-minded, their enigmatic legacies persist, challenging each new generation to unravel the mysteries left by those who walked the clandestine corridors before them.

Defining Purpose and Vision for Your New Secret Society

The creation of a secret society is more than a commitment to clandestine meetings and the cultivation of exclusive membership; it is an exercise in purposeful visioning. A society without a clear objective is like a compass without a needle, directionless and aimless. Therefore, the cornerstone of any enduring secret society is the clarity of its purpose and the sharpness of its vision.

1. The Genesis of Purpose

Before a secret society can take its first step, it must understand the 'why' of its existence. Purpose is the society's raison d'être, the deep-seated reason that will guide its actions and strategies. The founders must engage in introspective and forward-thinking dialogue to uncover this central driving force.

The Role of Passion and Interests: A society's purpose often germinates from the shared passions and interests of its founding members. Whether it be literature, philosophy, social activism, or simply the thrill of the enigmatic, this common ground serves as fertile soil for the society's purpose.

Addressing a Need: A secret society may also arise from the necessity to address an unmet need within the campus or community. This need could be for a supportive space to explore controversial ideas, a haven for artistic expression, or a network to foster academic excellence.

2. Sculpting the Vision

With the purpose as its seed, the society must then envision the full-grown tree—its ideal future state. A well-articulated vision provides a long-term perspective and sets a framework for the society's growth and the strategies it will employ to get there.

Imagining the Impact: What footprint does the society wish to leave on its members, campus, and perhaps the world at large? Envisioning this impact helps to refine the society's objectives and align its activities.

Crafting Traditions and Legacy: A part of the society's vision is often rooted in the traditions it establishes and the legacy it aspires to build. These traditions become the rituals that strengthen bonds and the stories that will be passed down as a testament to the society's existence.

3. Articulating the Mission

A mission statement bridges the gap between purpose and vision. It is a concise expression of what the society intends to do to fulfill its purpose and achieve its vision.

Simplicity and Clarity: A mission statement should be straightforward and easy to understand. It should resonate with all members and provide a clear direction for the society's activities.

Action-Oriented: The mission must inspire action and commitment. It's not just a declaration but a call to arms, rallying members to the society's cause.

4. Aligning with Core Values

Core values are the ethical compass of the society. They are the non-negotiable principles that dictate how the society and its members will behave and make decisions.

Identifying Key Values: Honesty, loyalty, bravery, wisdom—these are just examples of values a society might uphold. The key is to choose those that are inextricably linked to the society's purpose and vision.

Living the Values: Values should not just be stated but lived by every member. They must be woven into the society's fabric, from initiation rites to day-to-day interactions.

5. Developing a Symbolic Identity

A secret society often has symbols that encapsulate its purpose and vision. These symbols serve as a constant reminder of the society's identity and objectives.

Designing Insignia: Whether it's a logo, a seal, or a totem, this visual emblem represents the society's essence. It should be designed thoughtfully to reflect the society's character and aspirations.

Creating a Mythos: Beyond physical symbols, a society often develops a rich narrative or mythology that embeds its purpose and vision into a larger, often more enigmatic context, enhancing the allure and depth of its identity.

6. Structuring for Success

With purpose, vision, mission, values, and identity in hand, the society must consider its structure. How will it organize itself to best achieve its objectives?

Leadership and Hierarchy: Will the society adopt a flat structure where all members are equal, or will it have a hierarchy that defines roles and responsibilities?

Sustainability and Growth: The structure must also take into account the society's longevity—how it will recruit new members, pass on knowledge, and ensure its survival beyond the founders' tenure.

7. Planning for Challenges
A secret society must be prepared to face challenges and obstacles that may come from within or outside its circle.

Anticipating Resistance: From campus administration to public perception, a secret society may encounter opposition. Strategies must be in place to mitigate these challenges while staying true to the society's objectives.

Internal Conflicts: The society must also have mechanisms for resolving disputes and ensuring that internal dynamics do not derail its purpose and vision.

The objective of forming a secret society is a complex tapestry woven from the threads of purpose, vision, mission, values, identity, structure, and foresight. It requires thoughtful deliberation and steadfast commitment. When these elements are aligned, the society becomes more than a group shrouded in mystery—it becomes a transformative force with the potential to leave an indelible mark on its members and the annals of its environment. As with any institution, the true measure of its success will ultimately be reflected in the lives it touches and the change it engenders.

Creating the Mission Statement for Your Secret Society

The mission statement is the compass by which a secret society navigates the tides of its existence. It articulates the society's core purpose and vision, serving both as a rallying cry for its members and as the enigmatic facade presented to the outside world. This chapter will guide you through the nuanced art of crafting a mission statement that resonates with the ethos of your society and solidifies the collective identity.

The Essence of a Mission Statement

A mission statement, succinct and potent, must encapsulate the quintessence of your society's goals, values, and raison d'être. It is a declaration of intent, a beacon that guides your society's actions, decisions, and rituals.

Reflecting on Your Society's Core

Identifying Your Core Values: Begin by exploring the fundamental principles that your society will uphold. Is it knowledge, secrecy, altruism, power, or perhaps a blend of these elements? Establishing these values lays the groundwork for your mission.

Defining Your Purpose: What is the ultimate goal of your society? Are you aiming to influence, to protect a legacy, to foster personal growth among members, or to operate as a force for social change?

Articulation of Vision

Envisioning the Future: Imagine where you see your society in 5, 10, or 50 years. This long-term vision will not only inspire but will also provide a strategic direction.

Setting the Scope: Decide how broad or narrow your society's reach will be. Will your activities be confined to a single institution, or do you aspire to a wider influence?

Crafting the Statement

The Power of Words: Each word in your mission statement must be chosen with precision, carrying depth and resonance. Use language that inspires but also retains a shroud of mystique, befitting a secret society.

Balance of Clarity and Secrecy: While the mission should be clear to members, it should also maintain the allure of secrecy that is intrinsic to the nature of a covert organization.

Examples and Inspiration

Analyzing Historical Societies: Draw inspiration from the mission statements of historical secret societies.

Note how they convey their purpose while maintaining an air of mystery.

Modern Interpretations: Consider how modern secret organizations phrase their missions. Although less shrouded in mystery due to a more open society, their statements still hold a certain gravity and vagueness.

Iteration and Refinement

Drafting and Feedback: Create several drafts and solicit feedback from founding members. A mission statement should be a collective affirmation, not the vision of a single individual.

Refinement: Refine the statement until it strikes the perfect chord between enigma and clarity, embodying the essence of your society's aspirations.

Embedding the Mission

Living the Statement: Your mission statement should be more than just words. It must be lived and breathed by every member, embedded in every ritual, and reflected in all actions taken by the society.

Secrecy and Symbolism: Consider encoding your mission statement in symbols or a cryptic script to deepen the sense of mystery and commitment to the society's secrets.

The Mission as a Guiding Star

Decision-Making: Use the mission statement to guide all decisions made by the society, ensuring that actions align with the stated purpose and values.

Adapting to Change: Be prepared to revisit and adapt the mission statement as the society evolves. The core may remain the same, but its expression might change with time and circumstance.

Crafting a mission statement for your secret society is a profound undertaking that requires introspection, creativity, and a deep understanding of the society's collective heartbeat. It must strike a delicate balance between being an open declaration and a guarded secret, between the reality of the present and the vision of the future. In the shadows of your society's covert meetings, the mission statement will serve as an eternal flame, illuminating the path forward while casting intriguing shadows that protect your enigma.

Remember, the true power of a mission statement lies not in its words, but in the unity and purpose it inspires among the members. It is the silent pulse that synchronizes the heartbeat of the society, the unspoken vow that binds the individual to the collective quest. Let the mission statement be the cryptic seal that marks your society's passage through time, a legacy etched not just in documents, but in the indelible spirit of its members.

The Role of Mystique in Member Recruitment

In the realm of secret societies, mystique is not merely a veil of secrecy but a magnetic force that draws individuals to its enigma. Member recruitment hinges on this allure, promising a journey into the unknown. This chapter delves into harnessing mystique as a pivotal tool in attracting and selecting members for your secret society.

Understanding Mystique

Mystique Defined: Mystique is the subtle art of arousing interest through mystery and intrigue. It is an essential ingredient in setting a secret society apart from the mundanity of everyday associations.

The Allure of the Hidden: Humans are naturally curious creatures, drawn to the concealed and the unexplained. This curiosity fuels the mystique that secret societies can capitalize on.

Crafting the Mystique

Curating an Aura: The image your society projects should evoke a sense of intrigue and exclusivity. The symbols, language, and rituals employed contribute to this aura.

The Mythos: Develop a compelling narrative or backstory for your society, rich with lore and symbolism. This mythos is the cornerstone of your society's mystique.

Recruitment Strategies

Whisper Campaigns: Discreetly spread the word about your society through a whisper campaign. The less that is said, the more people will talk.

Selective Visibility: Appear in public just enough to be noticed but not enough to be understood. Leave a trace that sparks curiosity without satisfying it.

The Selection Process

The Veil of Secrecy: Prospective members should not be fully privy to the inner workings of the society until they have proven themselves. This partial knowledge creates a tantalizing lure.

Testing Commitment: Design initiation trials or tasks that assess not only the candidate's desire to join but also their compatibility with the society's ethos.

Use of Symbols and Codes

Enigmatic Branding: Employ symbols and codes that require interpretation, allowing prospective members to engage with the society's mystique intellectually.

Cryptic Invitations: Invite potential members using cryptic messages that hint at deeper meanings, suggesting that initiation is but the beginning of their deciphering journey.

Telling Signs of a Fit

Sensitivity to Subtlety: Look for individuals who exhibit an appreciation for nuance and can read between the lines—traits essential for navigating a secret society.

A Discreet Demeanor: Candidates should value discretion and possess the ability to keep the society's secrets sacrosanct.

The Role of Existing Members

Ambassadors of Mystique: Current members should embody the society's mystique in their demeanor and actions, serving as enigmatic ambassadors to the outside world.

Gatekeepers of Secrets: Members are the gatekeepers, carefully evaluating who is worthy of being entrusted with the society's knowledge and mission.

Social Proof and Exclusivity

Leveraging Influence: Having influential members can elevate the society's desirability, but this must be balanced with maintaining a diverse and committed membership base.

The Illusion of Scarcity: Create an illusion of scarcity in membership slots. The perception of exclusivity can increase desirability among potential recruits.

Communication and Rumor Control

Managing the Narrative: While mystique is valuable, it's essential to manage rumors that could misrepresent the society's purpose.

The Power of Silence: Sometimes, saying nothing at all can be the most potent tool in your arsenal, allowing others to fill the silence with their fantasies about the society.

Building Long-Term Loyalty

Deepening the Mystery: Once members are initiated, gradually reveal deeper layers of the society's secrets, ensuring their sustained interest and loyalty.

Cultivating a Legacy: Encourage members to contribute to the society's lore, thereby investing them further in the perpetuation of its mystique.

The mystique of a secret society is not just a shield that protects it from the prying eyes of the outside world but also a beacon that attracts the right individuals. It is a silent language spoken in the shadows, an intricate dance of revelation and concealment that thrills and entices. Recruitment, guided by the deft hand of mystique, becomes not just a process of selection but an initiation in itself, beginning a journey into the heart of secrecy.

In closing, remember that mystique is a delicate balance—too little, and the society appears mundane; too much, and it risks being misunderstood or dismissed as mere fancy. Striking this balance is the art that will ensure your society attracts members who are not only intrigued by the allure of secrecy but are also aligned with the profounder purpose of your collective endeavor. Let your mystique be both the mask that intrigues and the mirror that reflects the inner truth of your society to those who have eyes to see.

Establishing Your Society's Identity Through Symbols and Traditions

The heart of a secret society often beats in the rhythm of its symbols and traditions. They are the DNA, encoding not just identity but also continuity and purpose. This chapter explores how to craft and integrate symbols and traditions into the fabric of your society, creating a unique and lasting identity.

The Power of Symbols

Symbols as the Language of the Secretive: Symbols speak where words cannot, conveying complex ideas in simple forms. They are the silent communicators of your society's deepest values and secrets.

Historical and Cultural Significance: The choice of symbols may draw from historical, cultural, or esoteric sources, imbuing them with layers of meaning that resonate with members and intrigue outsiders.

Crafting Unique Symbols

Design Principles: The creation of symbols should consider simplicity, recognizability, and scalability. They must be easy to reproduce yet distinctive enough to stand out.

Integration and Consistency: Symbols should be consistently integrated into all society materials, from documentation to regalia, to reinforce identity and recognition.

Traditions as Pillars of Society

The Role of Traditions: Traditions serve as the framework for the society's activities, reinforcing camaraderie and the shared sense of purpose among members.

Establishing Rituals: Rituals are powerful traditions that mark significant milestones, transitions, and achievements within the society. They serve as a collective memory and create a sense of timelessness.

Creating Meaningful Traditions

Inception and Evolution: Traditions may begin as a meaningful response to a significant event or idea and evolve as the society grows, ensuring they remain relevant and engaging.

Balancing Secrecy and Spectacle: Traditions should maintain the society's secretive nature while providing a sense of spectacle and ceremony to internal proceedings.

The Induction Process

Crafting the Initiation Ritual: The initiation of new members is a pivotal tradition that should encapsulate the society's essence and test the newcomers' commitment and alignment with its values.

The Passing of Knowledge: Symbols and meanings are often transferred through initiation, connecting the new members to the society's lineage and lore.

Celebrations and Commemorations

Marking Time and Achievements: Celebrations and annual commemorations provide rhythm to the society's life, marking progress and honoring its history and achievements.

Ceremonial Gatherings: Regularly scheduled gatherings, steeped in tradition, reinforce bonds and affirm each member's role and significance within the society.

Symbols and Traditions in Daily Practice

Living the Symbols: Encourage members to integrate society symbols into their daily lives in a discreet manner, fostering a continuous connection with the society.

Personal and Collective Rituals: Develop personal rituals for members to perform, affirming their commitment to the society's principles, as well as collective rituals that strengthen group identity.

The Continuity of Traditions

Documentation and Transmission: Record traditions and the stories behind symbols to ensure they are accurately passed down through generations of society members.

The Guardians of Tradition: Assign stewards within the society to oversee the preservation and practice of traditions, ensuring their integrity and continuity.

Innovating Without Losing Essence

Adapting to Change: Allow traditions to evolve organically with the society's growth, ensuring they remain relevant and meaningful to all members.

Innovation Within Boundaries: While innovation is vital, it is essential to maintain the core essence of the society's identity through its symbols and traditions.

The Inclusivity of Symbols and Traditions

Reflecting Diversity: Ensure that symbols and traditions reflect the diversity of your members, fostering a sense of inclusivity and collective ownership.

Unity in Diversity: Use symbols and traditions as a means to unite members from varied backgrounds, focusing on shared values and common goals.

Symbols and traditions are not merely ornaments of a secret society; they are its essence and its legacy. They bind the past to the present and pave the way for the future, threading members into a cohesive narrative that transcends time. Establishing your society's identity through these means is not a task to be taken lightly—it is a sacred duty that, when executed with care, can immortalize the society's principles and its collective spirit.

As we close this chapter, reflect on the symbols and traditions that you will choose to represent the core of your society. Remember, they are the stars by which your society will navigate the future, the anchors that will hold fast against the tides of change, and the flames that will light the paths of those who will walk in your footsteps. Choose wisely, for these symbols and traditions will become the heralds of your identity and the guardians of your legacy.

How Greek Fraternities Use Symbols

Greek letter organizations, commonly known as fraternities and sororities, are some of the most recognizable collegiate groups in the United States. The use of Greek letters as their primary symbols reflects a tradition steeped in the promotion of brotherhood, scholarship, leadership, and service. These letters serve as emblems of unity and pride, representing the ideals and values that the members collectively uphold. Each letter is not just a character but is imbued with profound significance, often linked to the organization's secret motto or creed.

When designing a new secret society it can be instructive to consider how Greek secret societies use them.

Crests and Coats of Arms

Beyond the Greek letters themselves, fraternities and sororities often adopt crests or coats of arms. These intricate symbols are replete with iconography that denotes the history, purpose, and ethos of the organization. Elements like stars, chevrons, or heraldic beasts convey attributes such as aspiration, protection, and courage. The coat of arms acts as a more detailed counterpart to the simplicity of Greek letters, offering a richer narrative about the society's heritage and aspirations.

Ritual Objects and Regalia

Many Greek societies have ritual objects that carry symbolic meanings, such as paddles, stoles, or rings. These items are often personalized and passed down through generations of members, carrying with them stories and memories that reinforce the bonds between alumni and current members. Regalia, such as sashes, cords, or pins, is worn with ceremonial gravity and serves to identify and distinguish members within the broader campus community.

The Badge or Pin

The fraternity badge or pin is a cornerstone symbol worn over the heart, signifying the wearer's lifetime commitment to the organization. These badges are typically designed with the organization's Greek letters and may include precious stones, the fraternity's colors, and other symbols such as crosses or skulls, depending on the society's traditions. The badge is often revealed only upon the completion of the initiation process, marking a member's full entry into the society's inner circle.

Secret Handshakes and Gestures

Handshakes and gestures are perhaps the most personal symbols within a Greek society, often known only to initiated members. These acts serve as silent affirmations of membership and solidarity, whether members are within the protected confines of their chapter house or out in the wider world. The specificity of the grip or gesture ensures that only true members can successfully identify one another, maintaining the integrity and exclusivity of the society.

The Importance of Discretion

While symbols are a source of pride for fraternity members, there is often a level of discretion practiced in their display and use. Certain symbols, especially those linked to the society's secret rituals or meanings, are not fully disclosed to non-members. This practice preserves the mystery and allure of the society, maintaining a clear boundary between those within the fold and those without.

Symbols as Educational Tools

For members, these symbols are more than just markers of affiliation; they are educational tools. Through the stories and values associated with each symbol, new members learn about the fraternity's history and expectations for their conduct as representatives of the group. This education is not confined to the initial induction period but is a continuous process that reinforces the society's teachings throughout a member's life.

In Greek fraternity secret societies, symbols are the threads that weave individual members into a cohesive tapestry. They are the silent language through which tradition speaks and through which the past informs the present. By bearing these symbols, members carry the weight of their organization's history and the responsibility to contribute to its legacy. As the visibility of these symbols endures on college campuses, so too does the influence of the Greek societies they represent, perpetuating a cultural heritage that has become a cornerstone of the collegiate experience.

Developing Your Secret Society's Lore

The mystique of a secret society often lies in its lore—an intricate web of stories, traditions, and histories that form its backbone. A compelling lore not only enriches the society's culture but also strengthens bonds among its members. This chapter explores how to craft a unique lore, document the society's chronicles, and utilize storytelling as a powerful tool for member bonding.

Building a Unique Lore and Backstory

Foundations of Lore

- Origins: Begin with the creation story of the society, which sets the stage for its existence and purpose. Incorporate elements from the society's founding ideals, the zeitgeist of the era, and the personal narratives of its founding members.
- Mythology: Create a pantheon of symbolic figures or icons that represent the core values and missions of the society. These can be entirely fictional or based on real historical figures associated with the society's ideals. You can also pull inspiration from the history of the locations for developing your societies' mythology. There may be existing legends and stories

centered around past events or noteworthy individuals that can be used for incorporating into the mythos
of your secret society.

- Traditions: Develop unique customs and rituals that
  members perform, each with its own backstory that
  ties into the society's larger mythos.

Integration into Society

- Alignment with Purpose: Ensure that the lore aligns
  with the society's objectives and ethos. It should
  serve as a metaphorical map guiding the society's actions and decisions.
- Dynamic Evolution: Allow the lore to evolve with
  the society, integrating significant milestones and
  achievements into the narrative.

Symbolism and Metaphor

- Incorporating Symbolism: Use symbols that are
  meaningful to the society's mission and embed them
  into the lore. Each symbol should have a story ex-
  plaining its significance.
- Metaphorical Layers: Layer the society's traditions
  and rituals with metaphors that reflect deeper meanings and teachings relevant to the members' journey
  within the society.

Documenting Your Society's History

Chronicling Progress

- Archiving Milestones: Maintain records of pivotal moments, decisions, and events that shape the society's trajectory. This can include founding documents, landmark achievements, and pivotal meetings.
- Membership Legacies: Document the contributions and narratives of prominent members, preserving the personal aspect of the society's history.

Preserving Documents

- Secure Archiving: Develop secure methods to archive the society's documents, protecting them from unauthorized access while ensuring their preservation for future generations.
- Artifacts and Relics: Collect and preserve physical objects of significance to the society's history, which can include regalia, writings, and gifts exchanged between members.

Accessibility for Members

- Limited Access: Determine who within the society has access to these historical documents, typically restricting it to trusted members to maintain secrecy. Many societies designate only one person as their 'keeper of secrets' but large groups may have several members devoted to this task.

- Educational Use: Utilize the documented history as a tool for educating new members about the society's past and instilling a sense of continuity and belonging.

The Role of Storytelling in Member Bonding

Narrative as a Bond

- Shared Myths: Use the society's myths and stories as common ground for all members, fostering a sense of shared identity and purpose.
- Ritual Storytelling: Incorporate storytelling into rituals and ceremonies, making the lore a lived experience for members and strengthening communal ties.

Storytelling Sessions

- Regular Recitations: Hold sessions where older members recount tales from the society's lore, allowing for the transmission of values and traditions.
- Interactive Narratives: Encourage members to contribute to the lore by sharing their own experiences and how they reflect the society's principles.

Impact on Cohesion

- Unity Through History: Build a sense of unity by highlighting the members' roles in the ongoing story of the society. Each member's experience is a continuation of the lore.
- Lore as Legacy: Instill in members the desire to be part of the society's legacy, motivating them to contribute positively to its lore and history.

The lore of a secret society is more than just a collection of tales; it is the soul of the organization. It instills a sense of mystery and gravitas, connecting the members not only to each other but to something timeless. By crafting a unique lore, documenting the society's history, and using storytelling to bond members, the society's narrative becomes a powerful tool for cohesion and continuity. As members engage with the lore, they become part of the society's living history, each with a role to play in its unfolding saga. This chapter provides the blueprint for creating a lore that is not just heard but felt, one that resonates with the society's members and immortalizes their shared journey.

Forming The Inner Circle of a Secret Society

Criteria for Membership Selection

The soul of a secret society lies within its Inner Circle, a group defined by the careful selection of its members. The choice of whom to include is critical to preserving the integrity and essence of the society. This is not merely a matter of filling ranks but ensuring the continuation of a legacy.

Aligning with Values

Prospective members should not only align with the core values and vision of the society but should also demonstrate a capacity for discretion and loyalty. They are typically individuals who exhibit potential for leadership, a propensity for service, and a depth of character that resonates with the society's ethos. Academic excellence, community involvement, and a certain moral grounding are often requisites.

Diversity and Complementarity

A robust selection process recognizes the strength in diversity. The Inner Circle should be a tapestry of talents and backgrounds, ensuring a richness of dialogue and breadth of experience. It's not just about who the individual is at present but what they can become within the fold of the society. Complementarity is also key; new members should bring something unique to the table, complementing the existing members and filling any gaps in skills or perspectives.

Secrecy and Suitability

Potential members must understand and respect the concept of secrecy inherent to the society. Their past behavior and current temperament should be indicators of their suitability in this regard. It's not enough to trust that they will not disclose secrets; they must also be individuals who can navigate the nuances of secrecy without succumbing to the pressures it might create.

The Art of Discreet Recruitment

Recruitment is a delicate art, balancing the need for growth with the imperative of secrecy. It's a dance of subtlety and strategy, executed with precision to ensure that only the most suitable candidates are extended an invitation.

Observation and Interaction

Potential members are often observed long before they are approached. Members of the Inner Circle may interact with candidates in various settings, gauging their personalities, beliefs, and reliability. These interactions, while seemingly casual, are critical to evaluating whether an individual is a right fit for the society.

Personal Invitations

When a potential member is identified, the invitation to join is usually extended personally and discreetly. This could be through a one-on-one meeting or a personal letter, in which the nature of the society is outlined just enough to pique interest without revealing too much. The approach is tailored to the individual, ensuring they feel personally selected and valued.

Maintaining Ambiguity

Throughout the recruitment process, a certain level of ambiguity is maintained. Questions may be left partially unanswered, and details are often withheld until the individual has demonstrated a sincere interest and commitment to the society's values. This not only protects the society's secrets but also serves to build intrigue and commitment in the recruit.

Induction Rituals: Balancing Ceremony and Secrecy

The induction of new members into the Inner Circle is a momentous occasion, layered with tradition and symbolism. It's a ceremony that must balance the theatrical with the confidential, leaving an indelible impression on the initiate.

Theatrical Elements

Induction rituals often contain dramatic elements designed to evoke emotion and convey the gravity of the commitment being undertaken. These might include the recitation of oaths, the wearing of ceremonial garments, or the use of symbolic objects. Such rituals are steeped in the history of the society and are meant to create a memorable experience that cements the initiate's loyalty and sense of belonging.

Ensuring Confidentiality

While the ceremony is designed to be impactful, it is also shrouded in secrecy. Only essential members of the society are present, and the location is often secluded and secure. Details of the ceremony are not written down but passed orally, ensuring that the ritual is kept confidential and sacred.

The Pledge of Secrecy

Central to the induction ritual is the pledge of secrecy. This vow binds the initiate to the society, impressing upon them the critical nature of discretion. The language used is often archaic and solemn, reinforcing the timeless and serious nature of the promise being made.

Integration into the Circle

Once the pledge is taken, the new member is gradually integrated into the Inner Circle. They are introduced to the society's traditions, symbols, and history. This period is as much about education as it is about initiation, with the new member learning not only the society's secrets but also their role in safeguarding and contributing to them.

Mentoring and Monitoring

A mentoring system is often in place to guide new members through their early days in the society. This mentor is responsible for monitoring the initiate's integration, providing support, and ensuring that the society's standards are upheld. This relationship is also pivotal in passing down unwritten customs and understanding the nuanced dynamics of the society's culture.

The Inner Circle of a secret society is a blend of the carefully selected and the meticulously initiated. It stands as the guardian of the society's lore and the engine of its operations. The members within it are not just keepers of secrets; they are the bearers of a collective identity that transcends time. Through the meticulous process of selection, discreet recruitment, and symbolic induction, the Inner Circle remains an enigmatic yet fundamental component of the secret society's continuity and influence.

Organizational Structure of a Secret Society

Roles and Responsibilities Within the Society

The backbone of a secret society's longevity is its organizational structure. A well-defined hierarchy and clarity in roles and responsibilities are paramount for the smooth operation and governance of the society.

Hierarchical Dynamics

Traditional secret societies often operate on a hierarchical model. At the apex, there may be a Grand Master or President, who oversees the society's overarching strategies. Below this pinnacle position are officers with specific roles, such as a Treasurer to manage finances, a Secretary to keep records (albeit discreetly), and various committee chairs to oversee different activities or initiatives. Each role comes with defined responsibilities, crucial for order and efficiency.

Division of Labor

Effective division of labor is essential. Members are chosen for roles based on their strengths and skills, ensuring the best fit for each responsibility. Some may serve as guardians of knowledge, keepers of secrets, or as mentors to new recruits. Others might organize events or manage communications within the circle. This division allows members to contribute meaningfully and ensures that no single person is burdened with excessive duties.

Operational Duties

Operational duties are those tasks required for the day-to-day running of the society. This includes planning meetings, curating rituals, managing society assets, or coordinating with external entities discreetly if necessary. Operational roles are critical, as they maintain the society's pulse and ensure it functions effectively without drawing outside attention.

Decision-Making: Democracy in the Shadows

Despite the clandestine nature of secret societies, many embrace democratic principles in decision-making. This allows for a fair and collective approach to governing the society.

Meetings and Assemblies

Secret societies may hold regular meetings or assemblies where decisions are made. Here, matters are discussed openly within the group, and decisions are often made by vote. While the society's leaders may guide the discussions, every member typically has a voice, ensuring a sense of ownership and participation.

Voting Procedures

Votes can be conducted openly, by a show of hands, or through secret ballot to protect individual opinions and ensure honesty. Some societies may employ unique voting procedures that align with their traditions, such as using symbolic items or conducting the process in a ritualistic manner.

Conflict Resolution

In instances where there is discord or disagreement, societies may have established protocols for conflict resolution. This could include debate, mediation by senior members, or a tiered voting system where certain decisions must pass through multiple rounds of scrutiny before being ratified.

Ensuring Continuity: Succession Planning

For a secret society to endure through generations, it must have a robust plan for leadership succession and the transmission of knowledge and culture.

Identifying Potential Leaders

Long before leadership transitions are needed, potential leaders are identified based on their dedication, understanding of the society's ethos, and leadership qualities. These individuals are often given additional responsibilities and mentorship to prepare them for future roles.

Transition Protocols

Succession planning includes established protocols that dictate how new leaders are chosen. This may be through election by the membership, selection by a council of elders, or through an apprenticeship model where the current leader personally grooms the next.

Record Keeping

While secrecy is paramount, the society must keep records of its history, rituals, and governance. These records, however detailed or symbolic, are vital for continuity. They are often kept secure and revealed only to those within the Inner Circle or those ascending to critical leadership positions.

Training and Mentorship

Investing in training and mentorship ensures that the society's traditions and operational knowledge are passed on intact. This is not limited to leadership roles but extends to all positions within the society, maintaining a consistent quality of operation and preserving the society's culture and secrets through generations.

Emergency Succession

The unexpected can occur, and a society must be prepared for sudden changes in leadership. Emergency succession plans are in place for such scenarios, detailing interim leadership structures and expedited election or selection processes to maintain stability and continuity.

The organizational structure of a secret society is the invisible framework that supports its activities and preserves its essence. By defining clear roles and responsibilities, adhering to democratic principles, and planning for the future, a society ensures its survival and prosperity. Through these shadowed ranks, a society not only operates in the present but secures its legacy for the future, allowing it to wield influence and maintain its mission across the arc of time. Each role, decision, and plan is a thread in the tapestry of the society's history, woven tightly to keep the fabric of secrecy intact and unbroken.

Maintaining the Veil of Secrecy

The success of a secret society hinges on its ability to maintain the veil of secrecy. This chapter delves into the intricate practices and protocols that underpin this discretion, ensuring the society's mysteries remain shielded from the uninitiated.

Communication Protocols for Privacy

In a world where information travels faster than thought, the confidentiality of communications is the first line of defense in preserving a secret society's clandestine nature.

Encrypted Messages

To mitigate the risk of interception, societies have historically employed various methods of encryption. The advancement of technology necessitates the use of modern encryption software for digital communications, ensuring that messages remain decipherable only by the intended recipients.

Use of Symbols and Codes

Symbols and codes have long been a staple for secure communication within secret societies. These can range from simple cipher systems to complex symbolic languages known only to members. This not only protects information but also strengthens the shared identity and bond between members.

Dead Drops and Physical Communication

The reliance on digital methods brings inherent risks of exposure. Therefore, some societies still practice age-old methods like dead drops – leaving physical messages in pre-arranged secret locations. This bypasses electronic communication systems entirely, greatly reducing the digital footprint.

Verbal Passcodes and Signals

In-person interactions often require authentication. This is traditionally managed through verbal passcodes or hand signals. These signals are subtle, agreed-upon gestures or phrases that can confirm a member's identity and affiliation without drawing attention.

Security Measures: Protecting the Society's Secrets

A society's existence is defined by its secrets, and protecting these is paramount.

Safekeeping of Physical Artifacts

Important documents, artifacts, or items of significance are often kept in secure locations. The whereabouts of these safes or vaults are known only to the highest-ranking members, often guarded by complex security measures.

Information Compartmentalization

Secret societies typically employ a strategy of compartmentalization, where information is distributed on a need-to-know basis. This limits the spread of knowledge, reducing the risk of complete exposure should any one member be compromised.

Surveillance Countermeasures

Aware of potential threats, societies may use counter-surveillance techniques to ensure meeting locations and member activities remain unmonitored. This may include regular sweeps for electronic devices, employing decoy operations, or using noise generators to thwart eavesdropping.

Cybersecurity

In the digital age, robust cybersecurity is non-negotiable. Societies must secure their electronic archives with state-of-the-art cybersecurity measures, from firewalls and anti-malware systems to intrusion detection software.

Confidentiality Agreements: Legal Considerations

While much of a secret society's protection comes from its members' discretion, legal frameworks can also provide a layer of defense.

Legality of Secrecy

The legal stance on secret societies varies by jurisdiction, but most democratic societies tolerate them as long as they do not infringe on public order or laws. Members may be required to sign confidentiality agreements that are legally binding, deterring the divulgence of sensitive information.

Structuring Confidentiality Agreements

Confidentiality agreements for members must be carefully crafted. They should delineate the scope of confidential information, outline the duties of confidentiality, and specify the duration of these obligations. Importantly, they must also respect the legal rights of individuals and not overreach into illegality.

Enforcement of Agreements

The enforceability of these agreements hinges on their reasonableness and compliance with the law. Secret societies may include clauses that stipulate consequences for breaches, which can range from internal disciplinary actions to external legal recourse.

Legal Entities and Compliance

Some societies choose to establish themselves as legal entities, such as private clubs or nonprofit organizations, to leverage additional legal protections. This, however, comes with the need for compliance with regulatory requirements, which may pose challenges to the maintenance of absolute secrecy.

Balancing Transparency and Secrecy

In certain jurisdictions, the laws may require a degree of transparency from organizations. Societies must navigate these requirements carefully, providing just enough information to satisfy legal obligations without revealing their inner workings.

The veil of secrecy is both an art and a science, necessitating meticulous attention to communication, security, and legalities. By employing advanced technologies, age-old practices, and legal instruments, secret societies can safeguard their existence from the prying eyes of the outside world. The measures outlined are not exhaustive but form the core upon which the shroud of mystery is maintained. It is this veil that not only protects the society but also enhances the allure and mystique that draw members into its fold, ensuring that the heart of the organization beats on, unseen but ever-present.

Developing New Rituals and Traditions

Rituals and traditions serve as the heartbeat of a secret society, providing a framework that binds members together through shared experiences and creating a collective identity that transcends time and space. This chapter examines how to craft compelling rituals, celebrate annual events, and incorporate historical and cultural elements to enrich the society's heritage.

Rituals are the dramatized expressions of a society's values and beliefs, performed with solemnity and reverence.

The Role of Rituals

Rituals reinforce the society's ethos, provide a sense of continuity, and mark the passage of members through various stages of their secret society journey. They serve as a powerful tool for instilling the society's values and fostering a sense of belonging and commitment.

Designing Rituals

When designing rituals, societies must consider the message they wish to convey and the emotions they aim to evoke.

Rituals should have a clear structure, with an opening, a series of actions symbolizing key values, and a closing that leaves participants with a sense of fulfillment and belonging.

- Opening: Sets the stage and prepares members mentally and emotionally for the experience.
- Core Actions: These are symbolic acts or oaths that members partake in, which often involve sequences that are memorized and performed with precision.
- Closing: Provides a sense of closure and reflects on the significance of the ritual.

Sensory Engagement

Effective rituals often engage multiple senses to create a lasting impact. The use of incense, specific sounds, visuals, or even the tactile sensation of unique objects can enhance the ritual's memorability and significance.

Secrecy and Exclusivity

The exclusivity of rituals, known only to the initiated, reinforces the allure of the secret society. Members are often sworn to secrecy, which not only protects the society's traditions but also enhances the personal value of the experiences to each member.

Annual Events and Celebrations

Annual events serve as temporal pillars for a secret society, providing regular touchpoints for members to reconnect, celebrate, and reinforce their collective identity.

Planning Annual Events

These events, whether they commemorate the society's founding, celebrate significant milestones, or honor patron figures or deities, require meticulous planning. They often include formal ceremonies, feasts, or other forms of group participation.

The Importance of Consistency

Consistency in the timing and format of these events lends a sense of predictability and stability, allowing members to look forward to and prepare for these significant dates in the society's calendar.

Inviting Alumni and Honorary Members

Events may also serve as opportunities to invite alumni or honorary members, reinforcing intergenerational bonds and providing a sense of the society's longevity and reach beyond its current active membership.

Incorporating Historical and Cultural Elements

Drawing on history and culture provides depth and authenticity to a secret society's rituals and traditions, rooting them in a broader narrative that can give members a sense of participating in something greater than themselves.

Researching and Adapting Historical Traditions

Many societies delve into historical records to adapt ancient rituals or to revive forgotten practices. Such research can lend credibility and a sense of timelessness to the society's activities.

Cultural Sensitivity

When incorporating elements from specific cultures, it's important to do so with sensitivity and respect. Societies must ensure that they are not appropriating or misrepresenting the traditions they adopt.

Educating Members

Part of incorporating these elements involves educating society members about their significance. This education can take the form of readings, lectures, or workshops that provide context and understanding of the traditions being practiced.

Evolving Traditions

While historical and cultural elements provide a foundation, societies are living entities that evolve. Traditions can and should grow and change as the society does, reflecting the current membership's values and the times in which they live.

The rituals and traditions of a secret society are its most cherished practices, encapsulating its spirit and legacy. They are the milestones that mark a member's journey within the society and the shared experiences that create a collective memory. By creating compelling rituals, celebrating annual events, and incorporating historical and cultural elements, a secret society can build a rich tapestry of experiences that will not only foster deep bonds among its members but will also ensure that its legacy endures for generations to come. This careful curation of customs and celebrations is what ultimately weaves the intricate social fabric that binds members to the society and to each other in a world that remains unseen by those outside its circle.

Planning Secret Society Activities

The practical functionality of a secret society is tested in its ability to operate covertly, maintain strong internal bonds, and navigate conflicts discreetly. This chapter outlines how to plan and execute covert operations, foster camaraderie and trust within the group, and approach conflict resolution within the confines of secrecy.

Planning and Executing Covert Operations

Covert operations are the lifeblood of a secret society's active agenda. They are the practical application of its purpose and the crucible in which its secrecy is tested. Their phases can be divided into the following steps.

Strategic Planning

- Objective Clarity: The operation must have a clear and achievable goal that aligns with the society's mission.
- Resource Allocation: Assigning appropriate resources, including member talents and financial support, is crucial for the success of the operation.
- Risk Assessment: Understanding and mitigating potential risks, whether legal, social, or physical, must be a part of the planning process.

Execution

- Task Division: Assigning roles based on members' strengths and ensuring accountability.
- Stealth Tactics: Implementing measures to operate under the radar, such as using coded language and discreet meeting locations.
- Adaptability: Being prepared to alter plans as circumstances change.

Post-Operation Review

- Debriefing: Gathering all involved members to discuss the successes and failures of the operation.
- Documentation: Keeping records of the operations in a secure manner for future reference without compromising confidentiality.
- Learning and Adaptation: Using the experience to refine future operations and improve the society's operational capabilities.
-

Group Dynamics: Fostering Camaraderie and Trust

The cohesion of a secret society is dependent on the trust and camaraderie among its members. The secret nature of the organization heightens the need for solid internal relationships.

Building Relationships

- Shared Experiences: Regularly engaging in group activities that are both relevant to the society's purpose and enjoyable contributes to bonding.
- Transparency within the Circle: Fostering an environment where members feel safe to share thoughts and opinions freely within the society.
- Mutual Support: Encouraging members to support one another in society-related activities and in their personal lives strengthens bonds.

Trust-Building

- Confidence in Secrecy: Ensuring that all members are reliable in maintaining secrecy builds mutual trust.
- Dependability: Demonstrating consistency in actions and decisions helps build a foundation of trust.
- Respect for Boundaries: Recognizing and respecting personal and professional boundaries fortifies relationships.
- Maintaining Engagement
- Regular Meetings: Consistent interactions through meetings help keep members engaged and informed.
- Recognition: Acknowledging contributions and achievements of members encourages continued participation and loyalty.
- Inclusivity: Ensuring all members feel valued and included in the society's activities and decisions.

Conflict Resolution Within Secretive Groups

Conflicts within a secret society must be managed with discretion to maintain the integrity and unity of the group.

Early Identification

- Awareness: Leaders and members should be attuned to the early signs of conflict to address issues before they escalate.
- Communication Channels: Establishing clear and private channels through which members can voice concerns or grievances.

Mediation Process

- Neutral Party: Involving a respected member who is not part of the conflict to mediate can be helpful.
- Confidential Discussions: Ensuring that the conflict resolution process is kept confidential to maintain trust.
- Focus on Resolution: Encouraging a solution-oriented approach that aims for a win-win resolution.
- Reintegration
- Restoration of Roles: Ensuring that members involved in conflicts are reintegrated into their roles without stigma.

- Monitoring Post-Conflict: Keeping an eye on the situation to prevent recurrence and to heal any residual tension.
- Learning from Conflict: Using the conflict as a learning opportunity to improve society's protocols and strengthen its fabric.

Conclusion

A secret society in action is a delicate balance of clandestine operations, intricate human relationships, and the discreet management of internal conflicts. The ability to plan and execute covert activities successfully relies on the members' dedication to the society's objectives and their ability to operate with discretion.

Camaraderie and trust are the glue that holds the society together, ensuring that members work in unison towards common goals while also providing a supportive environment that extends beyond the society's activities. When conflicts arise, they must be managed with sensitivity and confidentiality to maintain the group's integrity and unity. Through strategic action, strong group dynamics, and effective conflict resolution, a secret society can thrive and achieve its aims while protecting the anonymity and security of its members. This careful orchestration of action, connection, and resolution underpins the society's ongoing success and perpetuates its mystique.

Developing Your Secret Society's Relationship to the Public

Secret societies, despite their insular nature, cannot exist in a vacuum. They must interact with the world around them to achieve broader objectives, from influencing policy to engaging in philanthropy, all while maintaining the secrecy that defines them. This chapter will discuss how a society can interface with its surrounding campus and community, carry out philanthropic activities anonymously, and cultivate a network of influential outsiders to further its goals.

Interfacing with the Campus and Community

Building Bridges

- Undercover Engagement: Participate in campus events and initiatives without revealing the society's identity, using members who are not publicly associated with the society.
- Indirect Influence: Impact campus life by encouraging non-member advocates to support initiatives that align with the society's mission.
- Alumni Involvement: Engage society alumni in advisory roles to guide current members in interacting with campus and community entities.

Collaboration

- Alliances: Form alliances with organizations and groups on campus, where the society's interests overlap with the public agenda.
- Subtle Sponsorship: Fund or sponsor events and projects discretely, without direct association with the society.

Maintaining Anonymity

- Proxy Representatives: Utilize intermediaries to communicate with campus officials and local leaders.
- Untraceable Contributions: Make contributions to campus and community causes in ways that cannot be traced back to the society.
- Avoiding Detection: Train members in methods to participate in public discourse and advocacy without revealing their affiliation.

Philanthropic Ventures: Giving Without Glory

Anonymous Donations

- Creating Shell Entities: Use legal entities to donate to causes that align with the society's values.

- Direct Assistance: Provide help directly to individuals or groups in need, ensuring that the act remains untraceable to the society.

Impact-Focused Initiatives

- Needs Assessment: Conduct thorough research to identify the most pressing needs within the campus and community that align with the society's ethos.
- Project Selection: Choose philanthropic projects that can make a significant impact while allowing for anonymous execution.
- Evaluation and Follow-Up: Monitor the outcomes of philanthropic efforts to ensure they are achieving the desired impact, adjusting strategies as necessary.

Educating Members

- Philanthropy Without Recognition: Emphasize the value of impact over accolades within the society.
- Skills for Stealth Giving: Train members in methods of anonymous giving and volunteering.

Cultivating a Network of Influential Outsiders

Identifying Allies

- Strategic Selection: Identify and approach potential allies who share the society's vision and can act as external champions.
- Values Alignment: Ensure that these outsiders align with the society's core values and understand the need for secrecy.
- Relationship Management
- Discreet Communication: Establish secure channels for communicating with these allies without exposing society affiliations.
- Mutual Benefits: Engage in a give-and-take relationship where both the society and the influential outsider gain from the association.

Leveraging Influence

- Policy Influence: Utilize the network to influence policy decisions discreetly.

- Community Impact: Leverage the network to make positive changes within the community that reflect the society's objectives.
- Expansion of Reach: Use the network to expand the society's influence beyond the immediate campus and community.

A secret society's interaction with the external world is a dance of shadows and subtlety. While the members work behind a veil of secrecy, their actions in interfacing with the campus and community, conducting philanthropy, and networking with influential outsiders define the reach and impact of the society.

Through covert operations and philanthropic ventures, a society can make its mark on the world without glory-seeking. By cultivating a network of influential outsiders, the society can extend its influence far beyond the confines of its immediate surroundings. This chapter lays the groundwork for secret societies to interact with the external world effectively, ensuring that their clandestine nature does not hinder their ability to effect positive change and advance their mission.

Financial Stewardship and Fundraising for a Secret Society

A secret society's success and sustainability largely hinge on its financial health and the prudence with which it manages its funds. The veil of secrecy adds complexity to this aspect, making traditional methods of financial management a challenge. This chapter delves into the practices of budgeting for clandestine activities, discreet fundraising and dues collection, and ensuring financial transparency within the trusted inner circle.

Budgeting for Secretive Endeavors

Secret Budgeting Challenges:

- Privacy in Planning: Financial plans must be made discreetly, with sensitive information limited to a select few to ensure that activities remain clandestine.
- Unpredictable Costs: Budgeting for secret activities may involve unexpected costs, requiring a flexible and adaptable financial plan.

Creating a Covert Budget:

- Assessment of Needs: Begin by identifying the costs associated with the society's activities, from routine meetings to elaborate rituals.
- Discreet Allocation: Allocate funds in a way that doesn't draw attention. Use general or ambiguous categories that mask the actual purpose when necessary.

Contingency Plans:

- Reserve Funds: Establish a reserve for unforeseen expenses, ensuring that the society can cover additional costs without compromising its activities or secrecy.
- Flexible Funding: Create a system that allows for the adjustment of allocations as the society's needs evolve over time.

Fundraising and Dues: Financial Contributions in Secret

Stealthy Fundraising Methods:

- Anonymous Donations: Encourage contributions that don't reveal the donor's identity, using methods like anonymous drop-offs or digital currencies.

- Private Events: Organize fundraising events that appear mundane to outsiders but serve the purpose of raising money within the society.

Collection of Dues:

- Regular Contributions: Set up a system where members contribute regularly to the society's coffers. This could be through direct deposits into an untraceable account or through trusted intermediaries.
- Dues for Discretion: Dues should reflect the need for discretion and the costs associated with maintaining the society's secrecy.

Soliciting External Support:

- Sympathetic Patrons: Seek financial support from non-members who are sympathetic to the society's cause and who value the discretion it requires.
- Philanthropic Backchannels: Develop backchannels for philanthropic contributions from alumni or like-minded organizations.

Financial Transparency Within the Circle

Limited Financial Disclosure:

- Inner Circle Oversight: Grant financial oversight to a select group within the society, ensuring that those who handle the finances are accountable to their peers.
- Segmented Reporting: Divide financial reports into segments that correspond with the society's internal structure, revealing only what each tier needs to know.

Accountability Mechanisms:

- Regular Audits: Conduct regular financial audits by trusted members to ensure funds are managed properly and to maintain trust within the society.
- Documentation: Keep meticulous records of all financial transactions in a secure manner, accessible only to authorized members.

Balancing Secrecy and Trust:

- Ethical Stewardship: Uphold ethical standards in financial dealings to foster trust among members that funds are being used appropriately.

- Communication of Financial Health: Provide general updates on the society's financial health to the wider membership without disclosing sensitive details.

Ethics in Financial Dealings:

- No Personal Gain: Establish strict rules against the use of society funds for personal gain to avoid conflicts of interest and maintain the society's integrity.
- Transparency with Donors: Ensure that donors understand how their contributions will be used, maintaining their trust while upholding the society's secrecy.

Financial stewardship within a secret society is a delicate dance between secrecy and transparency. Members must have faith that the society's funds are being managed wisely and for the collective good. Through careful planning, discreet fundraising, and an accountable inner circle, a society can maintain financial health without compromising its concealed nature.

By fostering a culture of ethical financial management, the society ensures not only its operational effectiveness but also the continued loyalty and trust of its members. This chapter provides the framework for establishing and maintaining financial practices that honor the secret society's need for discretion while upholding its financial integrity.

Growing the Secret Society's Influence Beyond the Campus

The longevity of a secret society often depends on its ability to reach beyond the immediate confines of its birthplace. Alumni relations, expansion strategies, and legacy building are crucial components that facilitate growth while maintaining the core tenets of the society. This chapter provides a roadmap for nurturing enduring connections with alumni, extending the society's influence, and crafting a lasting legacy.

Alumni Relations: Keeping the Flame Alive

Engaging Former Members:

- Continuity of Membership: Create a tier of membership that allows graduates to stay involved, albeit in a less active capacity, ensuring they still feel part of the society.
- Alumni Events: Host special events or reunions that cater to alumni, fostering lifelong connections and continuity within the society.

Communication Channels:

- Newsletters and Updates: Share newsletters or up-dates with alumni, keeping them informed and engaged with the society's progress and activities. Many secret societies even use digital newsletters, such as email groups or Discord servers, to keep in touch with their members and facilitate communication between them.
- Secure Platforms: Utilize secure digital platforms for communication that respect the society's confidentiality while allowing alumni to stay connected.

Leveraging Alumni Expertise:

- Mentorship Programs: Establish mentorship programs where alumni provide guidance and support to current members, enhancing the society's intellectual and social capital.
- Alumni Advisory Board: Consider forming an alumni advisory board to offer strategic guidance and aid in decision-making processes.

Expanding Your Society's Reach

Branching Out Geographically:

- Satellite Circles: Form smaller, affiliated circles at other campuses or in different cities, ensuring the society's ethos and objectives are preserved while extending its reach.
- Partnering with Like-minded Groups: Forge alliances with similar societies or organizations to expand the society's influence and resource pool.

Cultivating a Global Network:

- International Connections: Encourage international exchanges or collaborations, creating a global network that enriches the society's cultural diversity.
- Digital Presence: Establish a secure but robust digital presence that can facilitate international communication and virtual participation.

Diversifying Activities:

- Collaborative Projects: Initiate projects that require collaboration with external groups or societies, increasing the society's visibility and impact.
- Public Initiatives: Engage in public initiatives under anonymous titles, allowing the society to influence its surroundings while remaining in the shadows.

Leaving a Legacy: Preparing for the Society's Future

Documenting the Society's Evolution:

- Archiving Achievements: Maintain a private archive of the society's achievements, history, and notable members, serving as a source of inspiration for future generations.
- Legacy Projects: Implement legacy projects that have long-term impacts, ensuring the society's influence endures.

Succession Planning:

- Training Future Leaders: Invest in leadership development programs within the society, preparing members to assume higher roles and responsibilities.
- Continuity Protocols: Develop protocols that ensure the seamless transition of knowledge and authority from one generation of leaders to the next.

Institutional Memory:

- Oral Histories and Records: Encourage the recording of oral histories and detailed records, safeguarding the society's institutional memory against the passage of time.

- Confidential Time Capsules: Create confidential time capsules to be opened by future members, linking the past, present, and future of the society.

Philanthropic Foundations:

- Endowments and Scholarships: Establish endowments or scholarships in the society's name, contributing to the community and cementing the society's philanthropic legacy.
- Secrecy in Philanthropy: Engage in philanthropy with discretion, ensuring that the society's charitable actions speak louder than its need for recognition.

For a secret society to truly flourish and leave an indelible mark, it must grow beyond the campus that saw its inception. Fostering strong alumni relations, expanding its influence strategically, and focusing on legacy building are pivotal to its development. By implementing the strategies outlined in this chapter, a secret society can maintain its secretive allure while contributing to a broader canvas, ensuring its flame burns brightly for generations to come.

Through thoughtful expansion and diligent preparation for the future, the society will not only witness growth in numbers but also in depth and scope, achieving a lasting legacy that transcends time and space.

Parting Thoughts: Things That Founders of New Secret Societies Should Consider

The secret society, by its very nature, is an enigma. Wrapped in the shroud of mystery, these organizations often draw curiosity, skepticism, and, at times, apprehension. However, beneath the cloak of secrecy, they harbor potential for profound impact, both within their circles and in the wider world. This chapter seeks to distill the essence of ethical secret societies, reflect on their evolution, and consider their role as agents of change.

The Ethical Secret Society: Principles and Morality

Foundational Ethics:

- Integrity and Honesty: Despite operating in secrecy, the society must foster a culture of integrity and honesty among its members, ensuring that actions taken are not detrimental to non-members or the society at large.
- Beneficence: The society should aim for the good – contributing positively to its members' lives and, where possible, to the community and beyond.

Moral Accountability:

- Self-regulation: Members must hold themselves and each other accountable to the society's moral standards, practicing self-regulation to avoid the abuses of power and influence.
- Transparency Among Members: A level of transparency is essential within the society to build trust and ensure that the collective operates with ethical congruence.

Social Responsibility:

- Community Impact: The society should measure its success not just by the growth and loyalty of its members, but also by the positive impact it has on the community.
- Philanthropic Undertakings: Engaging in charitable work, while maintaining secrecy, allows the society to contribute constructively to societal progress.

Reflecting on the Journey: Evolution of the Society

Milestones and Growth:

- Charting Progress: Reflect on the society's milestones, from its inception to its current state, acknowledging both achievements and learning opportunities.
- Adaptability: The society's ability to adapt to changing times and members' needs is crucial to its longevity and relevance.
- Internal Transformations:
- Cultural Shifts: As the society evolves, so too may its culture, reflecting the shifting dynamics and perspectives of its membership.
- Legacy and History: The society's history becomes a tapestry, woven with the stories of past members and their contributions, shaping its identity and guiding its future.

The Secret Society as a Catalyst for Change

Power of Influence:

- Subtle Movements: The society can be a powerful force for change, influencing systems and ideas through subtle, often unseen movements.
- Inspirational Models: By exemplifying a model of integrity, camaraderie, and intellectual growth, the society inspires its members to carry these values into the wider world.

Cultivating Leaders:

- Leadership and Growth: Members often emerge as leaders, having been nurtured within the society's supportive and challenging environment.
- Ripple Effect: These leaders can effect change in their respective fields, the ripples of which may be felt far beyond the immediate reach of the society.

Reflections on Secrecy:

- Secrecy Revisited: The very secrecy that defines these societies can also be a vessel for introspection and personal development, fostering a safe space for members to explore and grow.
- Balance of Secrecy and Service: Striking the right balance between the necessity of secrecy and the desire to serve ensures that the society's actions remain honorable and impactful.

As we close the tome on the exploration of secret societies, we recognize that they are more than just keepers of concealed knowledge or orchestrators of clandestine meetings. They are a testament to the human desire for connection, for the creation of shared narratives, and for the exertion of influence. When anchored by ethical principles, reflective practices, and a commitment to positive impact, a secret society transcends the stereotypes of enigmatic elitism. Instead, it becomes a conduit for personal transformation and societal betterment.

The journey of a secret society is never static; it is an evolving narrative that demands constant vigilance and a willingness to adapt. The path tread by a secret society is laced with the potential for profound internal and external change. As each member contributes to the society's tapestry, they are interwoven into a legacy that, while hidden, is significant.

In the grand scheme, the secret society, guided by a moral compass, becomes a microcosm of possibility, a laboratory for leadership, and a sanctuary for strategic innovation. It is within the confidential confines of such a society that change can be conceived, strategies formulated, and leaders forged. As such, the secret society—enigmatic and shrouded though it may be—is not just a relic of a bygone era but a living catalyst for change, capable of leaving indelible marks on the canvas of history.

Appendices

Each of these appendices serves as a resource and inspiration for the creation and operation of a secret society, offering concrete examples and templates that can be adapted to suit the unique culture and objectives of a new organization. From solemn oaths to festive celebrations, the traditions and legacies outlined here provide a framework for the enduring allure and mystique of the secret society.

Appendix A: Sample Mission Statements and Bylaws

Sample Mission Statement 1:
"The Illuminated Scholars Society is dedicated to the cultivation of knowledge, the pursuit of enlightenment, and the fostering of brotherhood among its members. We commit to supporting each other's academic and personal growth while contributing positively to our community in secret."

Sample Mission Statement 2:
"The Arcane Circle endeavors to create a haven for creative minds to explore the arts and humanities. Our mission is to inspire innovation and collaboration while upholding the traditions that bind us in mutual secrecy and respect."

Bylaws Example:

Article I: Membership

Section 1: Membership shall be granted upon unanimous approval of the existing membership.
Section 2: Members must adhere to the society's code of conduct and maintain the confidentiality of the society's activities.

Article II: Meetings

Section 1: Regular meetings shall be held on a monthly basis and shall be mandatory for all members unless a valid excuse is provided.
Section 2: Special meetings may be called by the President with at least one week's notice.

Article III: Officers

Section 1: The society shall elect a President, Vice-President, Secretary, and Treasurer.
Section 2: Officers shall serve one-year terms and may be re-elected.

Appendix B: Ritual and Ceremony Ideas

Example Initiation Ceremony:

A candlelit procession into a historic campus building, where initiates swear an oath of secrecy and allegiance over an antique tome while wearing cloaks and masks obscuring their identities.

Example Annual Celebration:

The "Night of Whispers" where members partake in a grand masquerade ball, celebrating the founding of the society with intricate masks and a retelling of its history.

Appendix C: Case Studies of Historical and Modern Secret Societies

Historical Society - The Order of the Illuminati:

Founded in 1776, the Bavarian Illuminati aimed to promote enlightenment ideals and oppose superstition and abuses of state power. The group was eventually outlawed, but it has become emblematic of the concept of secret societies in popular culture.

Modern Society - The Skull and Bones:

An undergraduate senior secret student society at Yale University, known for its influential members and conspiracy theories surrounding its alumni. Established in 1832, its rituals and internal structure remain a closely guarded secret.

Cultural Society - The Freemasons:

One of the world's most famous fraternal organizations, known for its secret handshakes, rituals, and philanthropic activities. Its roots can be traced back to the local fraternities of stonemasons in the 14th century.

Glossary of Terms and Definitions Related to Secret Societies

This glossary provides key terms that would appear throughout the book on secret societies, offering readers a quick reference to understand and navigate the specialized language associated with such organizations.

Alumnus: A graduate or former member of an organization, often referred to in the context of college or university attendees.

Bylaws: The set of rules and guidelines created to govern the internal affairs of an organization.

Camaraderie: Friendship and trust among people who spend a lot of time together, especially within the society.

Ceremony: A formal event conducted on special occasions, such as initiations or commemorations.

Charter: A document that establishes the principles, functions, and organization of a society.

Cohort: A group of individuals working together for a common cause; in secret societies, it often refers to a specific class or generation of members.

Conclave: A confidential or secret meeting, particularly one held by the members of a secret society.

Constitution: A written document that outlines the fundamental principles and established precedents according to which an organization is governed.

Covenant: A solemn agreement between the members of a society to abide by the society's rules and secrecy.

Dues: Regular payments made by members to support the activities and functions of the society.

Hierarchy: The system of levels or ranks in an organization, where each level is above the other according to status or authority.

Induction: The process of formally admitting a new member into the society.

Initiate: A prospective member undergoing the initiation process.

Legacy: In the context of secret societies, it refers to long-standing traditions or members whose familial relations were part of the society.

Lore: The body of traditions and knowledge on a subject or held by a particular group, typically passed from person to person by word of mouth.

Mystique: An aura of mystery, awe, and power surrounding a person or thing, heavily cultivated by secret societies.

Oath: A solemn promise, often invoking a divine witness, regarding one's future action or behavior.

Paraphernalia: Objects and items associated with a particular activity; in secret societies, this often refers to regalia, symbols, and artifacts.

Philanthropy: The desire to promote the welfare of others, typically manifested by the generous donation of money to good causes.

Quorum: The minimum number of members required to be present at a meeting or to conduct the business of the group.

Ritual: A sequence of activities involving gestures, words, and objects, performed in a sequestered place and according to set sequence.

Secrecy: The action of keeping something secret or the state of being kept secret.

Society: An organization or club formed for a particular purpose or activity.

Succession Planning: Preparing for the future leadership of the society, often by training and selecting new leaders.

Tome: A book, especially a large, heavy, scholarly one.

Tradition: The transmission of customs or beliefs from generation to generation, or the fact of being passed on in this way.

About the Editor

Carey Martell was born on December 23rd, 1982 in Newberg, Oregon. As an autodidact Carey has studied history, philosophy, sciences and other subjects mentioned in this book since he was a small boy.

When Carey was seventeen, he enlisted into the US military, first in the National Guard of Oregon in 2000, and later re-enlisting into the active component of the US Army. He served a tour of duty during Operation Iraqi Freedom from 2003 to 2004. Carey was medically discharged from the US Army in January 2005 after suffering complications from the second round of anthrax vaccine injections administrated to him.

Carey spent the next several years of his life traveling around the US, living in numerous states, and making friends and acquaintances across the country. He briefly studied in the film program of Washtenaw Community College in Ann Arbor, Michigan and then later studied film production again for a brief time at Northwest Vista in San Antonio, Texas. Carey also completed an entrepreneurial accelerator program at Tech Ranch in Austin, Texas.

Carey has founded and sold technology startups in the video streaming and new media industry, and he has also published a number of books through his imprint, Martell Books.